FOUR BLACK REVOLUTIONARY PLAYS

Books by LeRoi Jones

Poetry
Preface to a Twenty Volume Suicide Note
The Dead Lecturer
Black Art
Black Magic 61-67

Essays
Blues People
Home: Social Essays
Black Music

Fiction
The System of Dante's Hell

Short Stories
Tales

Plays
Dutchman
The Slave
The Baptism
The Toilet
Arm Yrself or Harm Yrself

Four
Black Revolutionary Plays

ALL PRAISES TO THE BLACK MAN

LeRoi Jones

The Bobbs-Merrill Company
Indianapolis and New York

The Bobbs-Merrill Company, Inc.
A Subsidiary of Howard W. Sams & Co., Inc. Publishers
Indianapolis · Kansas City · New York

Contents

Introduction

a

What can I tell you about the world that you dont already know. Nothing. You know everything. You are everybody. You thought it up before I said it. Sure. You knew it all the time. So why even bother to read the plays. Just go on with the bullshit you call your life. Unless you killing white people, killing the shit they've built, dont read this shit, you wont like it, and it sure wont like you.

b

Trees talk death stones fly meat kills
the key is life in a sun face eye growing devils and angels

the balance is nigger-leroys
the change is the egyptian phenomenon
the change from black to white reversed is the change
    from white to black

the cities of the continent will change hands
the power on the continent will change hands

get in touch with Madbear
"hello, mad bear, whats happening?"

get in touch with Karenga and Tierinja
"Hey Now, Hey now, Habari Gani"

get in touch with the change, right now, athlete
the statues change from white to black
we are winners and we will win from these devils all this
    land

this is an introduction to a book of plays
i am prophesying the death of white people in this land
i am prophesying the triumph of black life in this land,
    and over all the world

Introduction

we are building publishing houses, and newspapers, and
    armies, and factories
we will change the world before your eyes,
                         izm-el-azam,
                         yes, say it,
                         say it
          sweet nigger
       i believe in black allah
          governor of creation
          Lord of the Worlds

                   As Salaam Alaikum
                   Ameer Baraka
                   1968

FOUR BLACK REVOLUTIONARY PLAYS

Experimental Death Unit #1

1964

For a used to be dead sister

Experimental Death Unit #1 was first performed at the St. Mark's Playhouse, New York City, on March 1, 1965, with the following cast:

Duff, a white man	Dude looked like Steve McQueen
Loco, a white man	Gary Haynes
Woman	Barbara Ann Teer
Leader	James Spruill
First Soldier	Walter Jones
Second Soldier	Gary Bolling

The production was directed by LeRoi Jones, sets were designed by Dominik Capobianco, special musical effects by Milford Graves.

SCENE
(*Third Avenue. Late winter.*)

DUFF
(*Barely high on heroin, eyes batting*) Well, sufferer, my windows are as icy as the rest of the world.

LOCO
(*Whistling softly, and bobbing in his suede shoes*) Is that a form of compromise? From dancing, into the deep sleep of tolerance?

DUFF
A parade of motives. (*Going to look in someone's low window*) Any caution will sense the slant of the world. How to get in on what's, shall we say, out there. (*Laughing slyly*) There are bunches of good things to eat.

LOCO
So our music is time's, and the time of the motive is the time of realest consciousness. Music. Basketball. Staring in some whore's eyes.

DUFF
I'm sacred as anyone, and I say the world is to the man who will take it.

LOCO
And perhaps you are right.

DUFF
You're, unlike the nightingale, a sob sister . . . a helpmate to the weak.

LOCO
You disapprove of life.

DUFF
No. That's not true. You do not know what life, if my definition holds, the life of beautiful things . . . you do not know what it is.

LOCO
I despise beauty. What you mean by that. I hate these
fools who walk around and call themselves artists, whose
sole connection with anything meaningful is the alcohol
decay of their skins. Weak dope dripping out of their
silky little beards.

DUFF
You have no respect for the world. No understanding of
what is of value in it.

LOCO
I respect everything. Existence is self-expression . . .
artists are freaks.

DUFF
They are necessary for the world to continue.

LOCO
They are as necessary as anything else, as even freaks are.

DUFF
Don't you respect knowledge?

LOCO
Only when it means intelligence?

DUFF
The open sore! (*He raises an imaginary glass in toast*)

LOCO
The open sore, in the blizzard. (*Raises hand. Negro*
WOMAN *in blue slouch hat steps out of doorway. She is
staggering a little, wined up, with one stocking drooping.
She could probably have been an attractive woman, in
another life. About forty, still gallantly seductive*)

WOMAN
Ho, boys. (*She draws closer*) Hey babarebop . . . two
sports.

DUFF
What have we here?

WOMAN
I am a groovy black lady . . . fresh outta idea alley. You dig?

LOCO
I am, shall we say, a digger.

DUFF
But he is a homosexual, so you're wasting your time.

WOMAN
Oh . . . shit . . . one of them. Why you have to be walkin' around my turf?

LOCO
Aw, miss, I ain't no homosexual.

DUFF
I'm just eager.

WOMAN
For what? Your dick up my butt? (*Looks up, smiling*) Drizzle, drizzle, drizzle, drizzle, drizzle. Ah, drizzle. Go head . . . do that right, now! (*At them*) The weather. Your faces. My stories. What are they in terms of spirit? Aside from droopy personalities that will inhabit the street's longing. We whores. We poets. We wet buttocks in the face of God. We all look, and long, and sing.

LOCO
Consider me a ready youth. Made to be used, under and because of you.

DUFF
I differ, unfair lady, only in the sense of my use. I am to be used in all your vacancies. All those holes in your body I want to fill. I got meat and mind to do it with. I

mean out there in the street. I'll throw you down . . .
mount you, giddyap! giddyap! big-assed nigger lady! . . .
then I ride you right out through the rain . . . maybe
licking your neck.

WOMAN
You lick your mother's neck! (*Softens*) But lick mine
too. In this terrible charlieland.

DUFF
Are you what you look like?

LOCO
(*Shivering toward the* WOMAN) Is she what she looks
like? Why don't you shrivel in your seltzer-water come,
you arrogant knownothing. She's lovely. Her wet thighs
make prints under the skirt.

DUFF
How much are you charging, pilgrim?

WOMAN
I charge just what you owe.

DUFF
Owe?

LOCO
You fool, we owe everything. (*Falls toward* WOMAN *on his
knees, with high whimper, finally tears*)

WOMAN
(*Screams*) OWE! OWE! (*She grabs at* DUFF'*s balls.*)
Everything. What there is to take. (*Laughs*) From what
remains of your dwindling stash.

DUFF
You whore. What're you . . . symbolic nigger from the
grave?

LOCO

(*Turning to restrain* DUFF) Shut up . . . shut up. This is the time your feebleminded muse, and mother . . . dippy wife, brother should have screamed through the snot of their Wheaties.

DUFF

A whore. A black stinking mess of a bitch.

WOMAN

Eat me, you lousy democrat!

LOCO

(*Grabbing the* WOMAN's *legs, as he writhes, though genteelly, on the floor*) Help! (*Begins to lick her legs and other flesh*) Help! Help! Help us, nigger. Help us, slick pussy lady. Let me eat your sanity, gobble your gooky mystiques. Lick you. Let me lick you lick you lick you lick you. I'm in an icebox. Heat! Silence! No noise between your hams. Lick and lick. Help, hairy lady. Smelly lady. Blackest of all ladies, help me . . . us! . . . all of us!

DUFF

Get up, you immigrant louse! Spineless! (*Dragging* LOCO *under the armpits away from the* WOMAN) Get away from that greasy . . .

LOCO

I am right, Duff . . . let me go! I know what's needed. I feel it. (*Screams, long long barely human*) Please. I'm right. We die without this heat.

WOMAN

(*Regarding both of them haughtily, taking out marijuana, beginning to pull it up into her mouth, sucking deep*) Whhhh . . . shit, damn queers. Whhhhh . . . (*Sucking, fondling the joint*) Whhhh . . . shit. Fools.

DUFF

Shut up or I'll beat your head into some delicacy!

WOMAN

Dumplings and caviar. Ahhh! Maybe chase it with a little thunderbird! (*A little abstracted*) While I dry out my drawers, and rub out the stains. That would be good.

DUFF

(*Advances suddenly, striking the* WOMAN) You whore . . . don't get strange with me.

WOMAN

Ahhh man, the old folks talked about spirits. *The* Spirit! I'll go mystical when I goddam please . . . even while . . . and if . . . you get your big pimple face pushed up hard between my legs. I'll be off somewhere then, thinking about something that would make you mad. What I care about you? Huh . . . your mother and father eat meat with their hands. I saw them old Robin Hood pictures. You can't tell me nothin'.

LOCO

(*Recovering slightly*) I will kiss her. I will. I love her. I want to touch her.

DUFF

(*Holding him away*) For Christ sakes, you little wop spik kike, get up and stand on your own two feet. (*Half whispering*) I've opened a charge account in your name.

LOCO

(*Straightening*) And now you'll swear there's a God?

DUFF

Yes, friend. (*Letting* LOCO *up, and shaking his hand* . . . *brushing off his clothes*) You bet there's a god.

WOMAN

Yeh, I agrees to that. There's a God allright . . . but diggit

... he's a jive ass motherfucka'! (*Thunder and lightning, the storm increases. Loud and specific thunder*)

DUFF
(*Screaming in laughter*) You see ... you see ... Thunder thunder big heavy God. My God. God of my fathers.

WOMAN
(*Throwing her hands up with her mouth open for rain ... screaming at thunder*) Yesssssssssss. His God. His God. If that's all there is up there, then kill me now. If you can. If that's what you do. (*Pause a moment, now matter-of-factly to* DUFF) Shit, man, must be something else up there. Something else!

LOCO
Madam, madam ... I love you ... I want to roll around with you in calm afternoons ... remember that. But God is (*Pointing*) up there! And I believe He knows what's best.

WOMAN
I'm best! Me. My big black thighs. You lay in here and find out how much anybody else got to do with it. I'll fuck your eyeballs out. And your friend's too.

DUFF
The lyric venereal! All hail, the change, and sport of kings. Whoring! And so we'll follow ... maybe ... if your price is right ... that's cheap ... and your bed is warm ... and you have some nice things to tell us.

LOCO
Yes, if we do it ... we have a right to feel right too.

WOMAN
Give me some money ... and pile on ... champs.

DUFF
Where's your rooms?

WOMAN

No rooms . . . just that hallway. (*Backs into hallway*)
Come on in. (*Starts to undress*) Come on in. Strip down.

DUFF

No rooms? Then we don't buy. We don't need this kind
of sordid thing.

LOCO

Please, Duff. I've got something inside me that's got to
be put in her. Please. In the hallway.

DUFF

For God's sake . . . don't you value your birthright? In
the hallway, Christ . . . think on it closely.

LOCO

Not thought. Just move. Move (*Grabbing* DUFF's *face in
his hands*)

DUFF

(*Pulling away*) Then go, sink into that filthy pussy. You
do that. (*Turns to go*)

WOMAN

You come back, hypocrite. You want it as bad as he do.
(DUFF *stops, turns but does not return. Stands looking*)

LOCO

Lady, lady, lady. (*Goes, sinks down on her*) Help me.
Help . . . me!

WOMAN

O.K., daddy, O.K., you just do what you can. We'll see . . .
We'll see. (*He pushes his head under her skirts back in
the shadows of the hall.* DUFF *watches for a while squirm-
ing, then he begins to take off his pants, and the rest of
his clothes. He goes into the hallway and tries to pull the
other man off.*)

DUFF
Get off, you whore face . . . get off . . . the thing's hard . . .
I can't wait for your greasy pleasure . . . get off!

WOMAN
(*Screech-laughing, shouting*) Yeh . . . it's good booty . . .
you better fight over it . . . good good booty. Come on, tall
fella . . . you get in here and get your own tongue in. Yeh
. . . it's good pussy . . . it's very good pussy. Hahahahaha-
hahahahahaha!

LOCO
Wait a second, Duff . . . just a second . . . I'm ready to
burst . . . just a few seconds more. Please!

DUFF
No, you get up . . . you been there too long . . . I gotta go
. . . Now! (*They scuffle, with the screaming. Now there
are drums heard in the background, regular, like a mili-
tary march. Then there are singing voices. Finally,* DUFF
pulls LOCO *out of the hallway and begins to beat him with
his heavy boot. He clubs until the boy is bleeding uncon-
scious.*)

WOMAN
Kill him! Kill him! Yeh. Do it. (*Laughs.* DUFF *finishes,
then throws the shoe away and leaps into the hallway on
the* WOMAN, *who is still screaming "Kill him! Yeh. Do it!"*

DUFF
Now, I'll deal with you, woman. See how deep I plunge!

WOMAN
Yeh. You kill him . . . now we see . . . we find out . . .
(*Laughs. Now a group of long-haired bearded Negro
youths marches out with drums and marching cadence,
though they look weary and full of combat. At the front
of the group one boy marches with a pike on the top of
which is a white man's head still dripping blood. They*

stop in front of the dead boy's body. Then the LEADER
turns as DUFF *and the* WOMAN *are noticed.*)

LEADER
Come out of there!

DUFF
Who's there? What do you want?

LEADER
(*Going up to hallway*) Come out, or I'll send someone in
to drag you out.

WOMAN
Ahh, honey . . . it's just a soulbrother . . . don't worry.
I'll cool everything out. (*Coming out. Louder*) Hey y'all
. . . what's happening? (*She crawls out of the hallway.*
DUFF *comes out next, staggering a bit, and bloody.*)

DUFF
Who are these?

WOMAN
Hey, cats, what's to it?

LEADER
(*Looking the* WOMAN *up and down very slowly. He turns
and beckons at the other soldiers.*) Who are you?

WOMAN
Nobody, baby . . . nobody at all . . . Who are you?

DUFF
What do you fellows want? (*Sees head*) God! What's
happened?

LEADER
O.K.

WOMAN
O.K., what . . . what's happening, man . . . why you bein'
so cool? (*Other soldiers raise guns, begin shooting at the*

two.) Hey . . . who are you, huh? What you think you in to . . . (*Falls, terribly surprised, ignorant*) Who are you . . . huh . . . why you bein' so cool . . . ?

DUFF

Niggers! Niggers! Niggers! Niggers! Niggers! (*Falls; one of the soldiers comes over and makes sure.*)

LOCO

(*Stirs. Raises his head, unseeing*) A little pussy. A little heat, that's all. Jus' a little heat! (LEADER *comes over to him. Looks at him a long time*) Just heat. Let me like it in. I need it, baby. I need what you got to give me. Please, please give it to me . . . please. (*He falls, dead.*)

LEADER

(*Looking, and stooping to make sure the man is dead*) A little pussy. You bet! (*He signals to the army, and they straighten up. He gestures to one soldier, who goes over and cuts the white men's heads off. Another soldier fits them on two poles. The bodies are pushed in a heap. The soldiers are ready.*) Ten-hup forwardddd . . . march . . . (*They begin to leave. . . . Last troops leave. Overheard from last ranks*)

FIRST SOLDIER

Hey man, that bitch look just like your mother!

SECOND SOLDIER

Man, I'll cut your joint off if you start that stuff. I don't play them kinda games.

FIRST SOLDIER

Yeh, but you'll pat your foot! (*When troops leave, bodies are slumped together on stage for some seconds, singing is heard, and the counting of cadence. BLACK*)

The End

A Black Mass

1965

For the brothers and sisters of The Black Arts

A Black Mass was first performed at Proctor's Theatre, Newark, in May, 1966, with the following cast:

BLACK MAGICIANS:

Nasafi	Yusef Iman
Tanzil	Barry Wynn
Jacoub	Marvin Camillo

WOMEN:

Eulalie	Vionne Doyle
Olabumi	Olabumi Osafemi
Tiila	Sylvia Jones

The Beast	Bob Davis

The production was directed by LeRoi Jones.

SCENE

(Jet blackness, with maybe a blue or red-violet glow. Soft peaceful music (Sun-Ra). Music of eternal concentration and wisdom. Some lights come up, outline the three magicians. Three Black Magicians. They are dressed in long exquisite robes, one with skullcap, one with fez, one with African hat (fila). The outline of some fantastic chemical laboratory is seen, with weird mixtures bubbling, colored solutions (or solutions that glow in the dark).

NASAFI hums along with music, voice reaches out occasionally to fill the whole laboratory. Second magician nods his head, beats in tune, absentmindedly to the music and singing. Third magician intent on what he is doing, with a large book in his hand. He is bent over a mortar and is jamming a pestle into it, watching very closely. The other two also have things they are doing, but in a more leisurely, casual way.

> *Signs in Arabic and Swa-
> hili on the wall. Strange
> drawings, diagrams of weird
> machines. Music can fill
> the entire room, swelling,
> making sudden downward
> swoops, screeching.*)

NASAFI

These are the beauties of creation. (*Holding large bowl
aloft. It glows softly gold in the dim light.*) The beauties
and strength of our blackness, of our black arts.

TANZIL

Is the mass completed?

NASAFI

Not completed, brother, but the potion is ready. All who
taste it will dance mad rhythms of the eternal universe
until time is a weak thing.

TANZIL

Until time, that white madness, disappears. Until we have
destroyed it and the animals who bring it into the world.

NASAFI

Animals are ourselves. We brought those animals from
somewhere. We thought them up. We have deserved
whatever world we find ourselves in. If we have mad animals full of time to haunt us, to haunt *us*, who are in
possession of all knowledge, then we have done something
to make them exist. Is that right, brother Jacoub? (JA-
COUB *is lost in his meditations.*) Is that right, brother
Jacoub? (*Notices*) Jacoub. You're off somewhere. Oh,
back into that experiment. What is it you're doing?

JACOUB

Oh, the same thing, brother. Creating a new organism.
I've been working on this for some time.

TANZIL
We know. We watch you, and wonder. We wonder what
you're doing. And what you're thinking. Tho we know
anyway.

NASAFI
You deal in a strange logic, brother Jacoub. You spoke
once of time and we forgot about it. Now there are animals
who hiss time madness in the air, and into our lives. I had
forgotten (*Turns to* TANZIL) but now I'm sure it was you,
Jacoub.

JACOUB
Yes. It was my work. I told you about time. What it
meant. Why I was working in that direction.

TANZIL
Yes, you told us. We respect your knowledge, brother.
But time is an animal thing.

JACOUB
Animals do not know time. It is a human thing. A new
quality for our minds.

NASAFI
But deadly. It turns us into running animals. Forced
across the planet. With demon time in mad pursuit. What
good is that? What does it bring to us that we need?

TANZIL
We have no need for time. In fact, brother, we have hatred
for it. It is raw and stays raw. It drives brothers across
the earth. (*Pause*) I think it is evil.

JACOUB
Can knowledge be evil?

NASAFI
Knowledge is knowledge. Evil is evil. But all things in

the world are interchangeable. In the endless procession
of meaning.

TANZIL
You know this, Jacoub.

JACOUB
(*Turns to other magicians*) I know that we are moving at
thousands of miles an hour. In endless space. In black
endless space. And that this is beautiful reality. But I
also know we must find out everything.

NASAFI
We already know everything.

JACOUB
That is not possible.

TANZIL
We know everything, Jacoub.

NASAFI
What we do not know, does not exist. We know without
knowing, because there is nothing to know. Everything
is everything.

JACOUB
And so I will on where I am moving. Where my eternal
mind takes me. Into the voids of black space where new
meaning lives.

NASAFI
There is no new meaning. We are your brothers, and we
know everything.

TANZIL
It is a fool's game to invent what does not need to be in-
vented.

JACOUB
Let us be fools. For creation is its own end.

NASAFI
(*Laughs, low, rising to high hysteria*) We know the myths, Jacoub. We know the realities. We know what is evil and what is perfection. We know we are black and beautiful speeding through the universe at thousands of miles an hour. We know beyond knowing, knowing there is nothing to know. And knowledge is repetition, and the bringing forth again of things that were so anyway. Everything already exists. You cannot really create.

JACOUB
I am creating. I have created. I made time.

TANZIL
You made animals who vomit time. And we must destroy them. You know that.

JACOUB
I created. I brought something into space that was never there. I will crowd the universe with my creations.

NASAFI
Jacoub, you speak of a magic that is without human sanction. A magic that would rupture the form of beautiful knowledge of beautiful world—you speak a madness which I know you create yourself. You want something that will release this madness from within your sainted heart. Why do you punish yourself with such flights? You are black and full of humanity. Yet you move into the emptiness of godlessness. You are god, yet you destroy your heart with a self that has no compassion, with a self mind that denies the order and structure of the universe of human signs.

JACOUB
I speak of movement. Of creation. Of making. Of thought.

NASAFI
Then you speak of humanity. Of the human mind.

JACOUB
I speak of things, of knowledge that is beyond the human mind.

TANZIL
If it is beyond the human mind, how will you create it? You are the human mind. No more. Tho that is everything.

JACOUB
Those animals of time, tho they be evil, are creation. From beyond the human mind.

TANZIL
Not so. You made them. Human. You made them. And now they roost in the human mind. And by the human mind they will be destroyed.

NASAFI
It is evil to pursue creation even into the lost spaces of the universe. What you bring back will be of no benefit to man. Remember the old myths, brother. The forbidden fruit of madness.

TANZIL
Yes. Tho we turn earth into gold, and cause the sun's rays to turn our engines. What you call thought is the projection of anti-humanity. The compassionless abstractions, the opposites. The mirror image of creation, turned and distorted, given power, by the forces of good, tho these forces breed hell itself.

NASAFI
Jacoub. You are working at what task now?

JACOUB
I told you. Thought. The creation of new energy. Yes. New energy, and new beings.

NASAFI
What?

JACOUB
Yes, brother. I have created time. Now I will create a being in love with time. A being for whom time will be goodness and strength.

TANZIL
This is animal sense. This is a magic against humanity, Jacoub.

NASAFI
Those animals you created are evil. They are the breeders of time. What beasts will you call forth who love such evil?

JACOUB
I will create only one, my brothers.

NASAFI
One what?

JACOUB
A man like ourselves, tho different because it will be beyond the human imagination.

TANZIL
And beyond human feeling. A gross distortion of the powers of righteousness. (*Bright flames flicker in the background, and go down.*)

JACOUB
A man like ourselves, yet separate from us. A neutral being.

NASAFI
Neutral being. What madness is this? How can a being be neutral?

JACOUB
Neutral because we, I, have created him, and can fill him as I will. From beyond the powers of natural creation. I make a super-natural being. A being who will not respond to the world of humanity. A being who will make its own will and direction. A being who will question even you and

I, my brothers. A being who will be like us, but completely separate. Can you understand? (*Women run in, screaming. Writhing. Twisting in their thin garments*) Magicians. Magicians. Magicians. Ohhhhhh. Ohhhhhhh. Magicians. Black magicians . . . What fault has our life created? T—There is evil baking the sky. E—The stars are out in daytime. O—The night is filled with thousands of suns.

NASAFI
What? What is this? What are you women doing running into this sanctuary?

EULALIE
The elements disturb us, Lord Magician. The elements threaten us.

OLABUMI
The sky is not the sky. The earth trembles beneath our feet.

TIILA
The sea shudders and rages, and throws strange creatures on the land.

TANZIL
Jacoub. (*Advances toward him*) What is this? (*Consulting his book which he has dangling from his waist*) Do these things have to do with your experiments?

JACOUB
I have no way of knowing. What I do sets off things beyond our reasoning.

NASAFI
Of course it is your experiment. What do you hope to create? (JACOUB *is mixing his final solution. Lights go out. Blasts of flame. The women scream.*) Magicians. Why are we so frightened? There is evil riding in the air.

TIILA
Mad visions in the blackness. Oh no. Magicians. Take
care.

JACOUB
Now is the time of creation. I enter one solution in the
other. (*Screaming*) The blood flows in my head and
fingers. The world is expanding. I create the new sub-
stance of life. Aiiiiieeee. (*Bright explosion flashes and a
siren-like laughter blasting. . . . The laboratory is intense
red, then hot violent white. The sirens go up to ear-
breaking pitch. The women scream.*)

NASAFI
Jacoub! Jacoub!

TANZIL
Brother . . . Brother Jacoub . . . what have you done?
(*The sirens, screams, and blasting lights are sustained for
a few seconds, silhouettes against the white flames that
begin to dart around the laboratory. Another intense
explosion, the room is silent and dark, and then a sudden
hot white glare*)

TANZIL
Jacoub?

WOMEN
Oooooh . . . The earth is alien. Our mothers are sick. The
world has shrunk and is choking us.

NASAFI
(*Explosions*) Deathfire.

JACOUB
No, lifefire. Lifefire. My brothers!

TANZIL
Jacoub, I fear we teeter above the actual horrible void.
(*Now the glare, glowing wild bright, seems to split. The*

sound is like glass being scraped on a blackboard. A crouched figure is seen covered in red flowing skins like capes. He shoots up, leaping straight off the stage screaming, Sun-Ra music of shattering dimension. The figure is absolutely cold white with red lizard-devil mask which covers the whole head, and ends up as a lizard spine cape. The figure screams, leaping and slobberlaughing through the audience.)

BEAST

I white. White. White. White. (*Leaps, coming to stiffness, then screams stupidly*) White! White! White! (*Hops like beast goon, making horrible farting sounds with his mouth*) White! White! White! (*Hops back toward stage, and up*) White! White! (*As he leaps on stage, he begins to vomit terribly, licking his body where the vomit lands, and vomiting horribly. The women begin to scream uncontrollably. The smoke is clearing, and the white thing hops and shudders, vomiting occasionally, and trying to make other explanatory speech-like sounds, but all that comes out intelligibly is the same phrase.)* White! White! White! (*Then he gurgles off into unintelligible "explanations." JACOUB is standing stiff, watching his creature. Then he moves forward tentatively, his arms spreading. The creature still leaps and hops, tho now less violently, his cries growing to gurgles and slobbers. JACOUB is moving forward. The thing is still trying to frighten the audience.)*

JACOUB

Brothers . . . Brothers . . . Look at this . . . LOOK AT THIS . . . (*NASAFI and TANZIL are moving away from the creature and JACOUB. Both the magicians are drawing their capes up to the faces. NASAFI rubs his forehead and an eye appears in the middle of his forehead.)*

NASAFI

It is a monster, Jacoub. That's what you have made. A monster.

JACOUB
It is life, no matter, new life. And strange. Look at it.

TANZIL
(*Drawing his elder's whisk, he shakes it, speaking*) *Izm-el-Azam* . . . *Izm-el-Azam* . . . (*Repeats over and over*) A mirror of twisted evil. The blind reflection of humanity. This is a soulless beast, Jacoub.

JACOUB
We will teach it.

TANZIL
It will not listen. It has no feeling.

NASAFI
I looked into the wet corridors of the thing's heart, and there was no soulheat. Where the soul's print should be, there is only a cellulose pouch of disgusting habits. (*And with a sudden burst of emotion*) THIS THING WILL KILL, JACOUB . . . WILL TAKE HUMAN LIFE . . . (*And the last is long-drawn-out with the terror of the statement.*) Jacoub, this creature will take human life . . . because IT HAS NO REGARD FOR HUMAN LIFE!

JACOUB
Brothers, I have created another man.

NASAFI
No, Jacoub. You have created a soulless monster. (*The women scream. Suddenly the* BEAST *wheels around, facing the terrified black people. Horrible wheezing sounds, still pushed by the same "White" phrase, gurgle out of his fangs. Tall white bones almost pushing through the "flesh." A cave man's loincloth beneath the mask-cape. Sometimes shakes with hideous laughter, staring into its hands, which are webbed, as are its feet. When it is not vomiting it is chewing, and spitting, wheezing and scratching. The* BEAST *turns staring at the black people. Wheezing softly, looking in each face.* JACOUB *has stopped, but spreads his arms in welcome.*)

JACOUB
(*Approaching*) You ... are ...

BEAST
(*In weird parrotlike fashion*) You ... You ... You ...
(*Then goes into initial barely intelligible chant*) White!
White!

JACOUB
(*Pointing to himself*) I. Eye! (*At eye, gesturing*) Me!

BEAST
(*Stroking its own chest; slobbering smile crosses its face*)
Me! Me! (*A little hop*) Me! ... White! ... White! Me!
... White! (*A sudden burst of horrible laughter. Then
suddenly the monster turns and begins snarling, then
laughing. In high hysterical falsetto. Snarls. Laughs. Then
leaps at* JACOUB. JACOUB *waves his hand and freezes the*
BEAST *behind an invisible wall. Then the* BEAST *leaps at
the women, grabbing throats or trying to throw open their
robes and stick his head in.*)

TANZIL
(*Waves the elder's whisk and a bolt of lightning strikes
between the girl and the* BEAST) Izm-el-Azam! Jacoub ...
you have turned loose absolute evil.

JACOUB
How can there be evil in creation, brother? We will teach
this thing the world of humanity. And we will benefit by
its inhuman ...

NASAFI
Benefit? What are you saying? Jacoub ... you said it ...
this thing is the soulless distortion of humanity. (*The*
BEAST *is standing fixed by black magic, shuddering in
terror, but also in a maniacal attempt to free himself from
invisible bonds. He grunts his repeated "White," every
now and again punctuating it with a popeyed scream,*

"Me!" Now one of the young women, attacked by the monster, grabs her throat and begins to stagger.)

TIILA

Magicians. This thing has hurt me. My breath is short. My eyes are turning to stone.

NASAFI

Jacoub.

JACOUB

What is it? What's happening to you?

TANZIL

Oh, Dervish (*Head thrown back*), make us strong against this evil! (*The* WOMAN *stumbles toward* JACOUB, *her face draining of color. Her voice grows coarse, she screams, covering herself with her robes. She emerges, slowly, from within the folds of the garment, her entire body shuddering, and beginning to do the small hop the beast did. Suddenly she throws back the robes, and she is white, or white blotches streak her face and hair. She laughs and weeps in deadly cross between white and black. Her words have turned to grunts, and she moves like an animal robot.*)

TIILA

White! White! (*Her humanity breaks through the dead animal language briefly.*) OH LORDS HELP ME I AM TURNED INTO A MONSTER. OH LORDS HEEEE-EEEEELLLLLLLLL . . . (*And then she slumps, and begins to hop around, slobbering and scratching.*) White! White! White! (*The other women cringe and moan the woman's name.*)

WOMEN

Tiila . . . Oh Lord, Tiila . . . What has happened to her? . . . Ohhhh . . . evil, evil stalks us. (*The* BEAST, *seeing the woman change from his bite-caress, jiggles and makes obscene movements with his hips, overjoyed. He is still caught in the lightning cage.*)

NASAFI
(*Sends another thunderbolt, stunning the woman, freezing her like the* BEAST. *She moans softly, tearing her body in the trance.*) May heaven forgive you, Jacoub! May heaven forgive you! (JACOUB *is trying to minister to the woman. But she shrinks away and slobbers unintelligible curses.*)

JACOUB
Izm-el-Azam! Let the Lord speak to me. Tell me my error. (*In terror at the woman*) This whiteness spreads itself without effort. For the thing is sexless. It cannot breed.

TANZIL
It has merely to touch something to turn it into itself. Or else it sucks out the life juices. Look at our dying sister . . . producing its own hideous image.

JACOUB
Tell me my error.

NASAFI
Jacoub, your error . . . the substitution of thought for feeling. A heart full of numbers and cold formulae. A curiosity for anti-life, for the yawning voids and gaps in humanity we feel sometimes when we grow silent in each other's presence, sensing the infinite millions of miles in the universe, as finite as it is.

TANZIL
Asking God's questions, and giving animal answers! We are original reason, and you slip through darkness sliding insanely down those slopes of centuries, endless space, to where the only life is fire burning stone. The cold mineral world. And then, brother, we reach back to warmth and feeling, to the human mind, and compassion. And rise

again, back on up the scale, reaching again for the sphere of spheres, back to original reason. To where we always were.

NASAFI
You fell, brother. The monster's eyes are watery colorless. With endless space beyond. The thing inhabits the voids of reason. Its function was as horrible nothingness. As absence. Of feeling, of thought, of compassion. Out between the stars where life does not exist. This beast is the twisted thing a man would be, *alone* . . . without his human soul.

JACOUB
We will teach it to feel. To love. (*Growing animated*)

TANZIL
It cannot. An animal with its nose quivering.

JACOUB
But it recognized Woman.

TANZIL
Not as the black beautiful lady of our universe, but pure female spoor and meat. An animal with its nose spread open ready to pop the world.

NASAFI
Jacoub, what will you do with this beast? And now the woman . . .

JACOUB
Transport them into the interior laboratory, where I will teach him. The girl . . . there must be some way to restore her life.

TANZIL
This teaching idea is madness, Jacoub. What would you teach an evil spirit?

NASAFI
Yes, perhaps we should cast them out. Perhaps the cold
north where we banished the animals of time. In those
pits of the earth, the creature might be left to make some
horrible life of his own.

WOMEN
Magicians . . . what will you do? Tiila is turned into the
beast.

JACOUB
You women should not have invaded this laboratory. You
should leave now!

NASAFI
Were any more of you touched by this foulness?

WOMEN
No, Lord. Only Tiila. Only Tiila.

TANZIL
Jacoub. You cannot teach a beast. A blankness in humanity. And we cannot kill. We must set these things
loose in the cold north. Where they may find a life, in the
inhuman cold.

NASAFI
Yes. The beast . . . and sadly, the woman, must be cut off
from our people. These things are killers. And smell of
the pig.

TANZIL
Sing, women. Sing against this madness and evil. Jacoub.
Let the women create their gentle thing here, their rich
life smells. Sing, women. Against this sucking death we
see. Sing. (*The women, pulling themselves close to each
other, huddled in their fear, raise their voices, at first very
softly, with the purring of beautiful pussies. Then they
begin to shriek their songs (Sun-Ra songs), as if in terror
against the two white shivering things quivering in the
middle of the laboratory.*)

TANZIL
Sing, black women! Sing! Raise your gorgeous souls!

JACOUB
But brothers, we must have compassion, even for evil. We
must teach them.

NASAFI
Jacoub. I forbid it. You move against holiness!

JACOUB
No, brother.

TANZIL
Jacoub. You must leave these things in the cold.

JACOUB
But our own Tiila . . .

NASAFI
Look at her. She is not Tiila. She is the void. The evil of
blank cold licking the stars.

JACOUB
Even this terror. This inhumanity is conceived, you said,
by men. By myself.

NASAFI
There is no self but the breathing world.

JACOUB
And so we shut out part of that world. Part of our lives.
Part of knowledge. What is there to desire in the world
if we cannot speculate about what we would have exist
in it?

TANZIL
There should be no desire but the desire to do away with
desire.

NASAFI
This self. This desire. Time. And this white . . . monster.

JACOUB
Man.

NASAFI
Whatever you would call it. Though this thing is not a
man. We are men, brother. And this thing is not ourselves. But the hatred of ourselves. Our wholeness. And
this self you speak of, and this desire, and the animals of
hated time, now these horrible beasts, all these things,
Jacoub, set you apart from your brothers. And may God
have mercy on your soul.

JACOUB
No, brothers. I will show you. I will begin to teach them.
I will have Tiila back. Look. I break the spell and begin
to work . . .

NASAFI
No, no, Jacoub . . .

WOMEN
(*Their singing turning to screams of horror*) Masters.
Magicians. Lord Jacoub. What . . . ?

TANZIL
Jacoub.

JACOUB
(*Gesturing*) I will prove the power of knowledge. The wisdom locked beyond the stars. Izm-el-Azam. (*At* JACOUB'S
*gesture, the two beings spring into animation, attacking
the magicians and women, killing them with fangs and
claws.*)

JACOUB
(*Staggering under the attack, with last breath screams as
the beasts close in*) With my last breath I condemn you to
the caves. For my dead brothers. May you vanish forever
into the evil diseased caves of the cold . . . Forever, into

the caves . . . Izm . . . Izm . . . Izm-el-Azam. May God have mercy . . . *(Falls. The beasts howl and hop, and then, turning to the audience, their mouths drooling and making obscene gestures, they move out into the audience, kissing and licking people as they hop eerily out, still screaming*: "White! . . . White! Me . . . Me . . . Me . . . White!")

(NARRATOR'S *voice over loud speaker with low drums and heavy trombones after beasts leave*)

NARRATOR
And so Brothers and Sisters, these beasts are still loose in the world. Still they spit their hideous cries. There are beasts in our world, Brothers and Sisters. There are beasts in our world. Let us find them and slay them. Let us lock them in their caves. Let us declare the Holy War. The Jihad. Or we cannot deserve to live. Izm-el-Azam. Izm-el Azam. Izm-el-Azam. Izm-el-Azam. *(Repeated until all lights black)*

Black

Great Goodness of Life

A Coon Show
1966

For my father with love and respect

Great Goodness of Life was first performed at Spirit House, Newark, by the Spirit House Movers, in November 1967. The cast was as follows:

Voice of the Judge	David Shakes
Court Royal,	Larry Miller
a middle aged Negro man,	
grey haired, slight	Mubarak Mahmoud
Attorney Breck,	
middle aged Negro man	Yusef Iman
Hoods 1 & 2*	Damu
	Larry Miller
Young Woman,	
around 25 years old, colored	Elaine Jones
Hoods 3 & 4	Jenga Choma
Young Victim	Damu

The production was directed by LeRoi Jones, with lighting designed by Aminifu.

*Hoods 1 & 2 are KKK-like figures, Hoods 3 & 4 are more refined than the first two, wear business suits.

SCENE

(*Outside an old log cabin, with morning frost letting up a little.*)

VOICE

Court.

(*A man,* COURT ROYAL, *comes out, gray but still young-looking. He is around fifty. He walks straight, though he is nervous. He comes uncertainly. Pauses.*)

Come on.

(*He walks right up to the center of the lights.*)

Come on.

COURT ROYAL
I don't quite understand.

VOICE

Shutup, nigger.

COURT ROYAL
What? (*Meekly, then trying to get some force up*) Now what's going on? I don't see why I should . . .

VOICE

I told you to
shutup, nigger.

COURT ROYAL
I don't understand. What's going on?

VOICE

Black lunatic. I
said shutup. I'm
not going to tell
you again!

COURT ROYAL
But . . . Yes.

> VOICE
> You are Court Royal,
> are you not?

COURT ROYAL
Yes. I am. But I don't understand.

> VOICE
> You are charged
> with shielding a
> wanted criminal.
> A murderer.

COURT ROYAL
What? Now I know you have the wrong man. I've done no
such thing. I work in the Post Office. I'm Court Royal.
I've done nothing wrong. I work in the Post Office and
have done nothing wrong.

> VOICE
> Shutup.

COURT ROYAL
But I'm Court Royal. Everybody knows me. I've always
done everything . . .

> VOICE
> Court Royal you
> are charged with harboring
> a murderer. How do you
> plead?

COURT ROYAL
Plead? There's a mistake being made. I've never done anything.

> VOICE
> How do you plead?

COURT ROYAL
I'm not a criminal. I've done nothing . . .

> VOICE
> Then you plead,
> not guilty?

COURT ROYAL
Of course I'm not guilty. I work in the Post Office. (*Tries
to work up a little humor*) You know me, probably.
Didn't you ever see me in the Post Office? I'm a supervisor; you know me. I work at the Post Office. I'm no
criminal. I've worked at the Post Office for thirty-five
years. I'm a supervisor. There must be some mistake.
I've worked at the Post Office for thirty-five years.

> VOICE
> Do you have an
> attorney?

COURT ROYAL
Attorney? Look you'd better check you got the right man.
You're making a mistake. I'll sue. That's what I'll do.

> VOICE
> (*The* VOICE *laughs
> long and cruelly.*)

COURT ROYAL
I'll call my attorney right now. We'll find out just what's
going on here.

> VOICE
> If you don't have
> an attorney, the
> court will assign
> you one.

COURT ROYAL
Don't bother. I have an attorney. John Breck's my attorney. He'll be down here in a few minutes—the minute I
call.

>   VOICE
>   The court will
>   assign you an
>   attorney.

        COURT ROYAL
But I have an attorney. John Breck. See, it's on this card.

>   VOICE
>   Will the legal
>   aid man please step
>   forward.

        COURT ROYAL
No. I have an attorney. If you'll just call, or adjourn the
case until my attorney gets here.

>   VOICE
>   We have an attor-
>   ney for you.
>   Where is the legal
>   aid man?

        COURT ROYAL
But I have an attorney. I want my attorney. I don't need
any legal aid man. I have money, I have an attorney. I
work in the Post Office. I'm a supervisor; here look at
my badge. (*A bald-headed smiling house slave in a
wrinkled dirty tuxedo crawls across the stage; he has a
wire attached to his back leading offstage. A huge key
in the side of his head. We hear the motors "animating"
his body groaning like tremendous weights. He grins,
and slobbers, turning his head slowly from side to side.
He grins. He makes little quivering sounds.*)

>   VOICE
>   Your attorney.

        COURT ROYAL
What kind of foolishness is this? (*He looks at the man.*)

What's going on? What's your name? (*His "voice" be-gins some time after the question: the wheels churn out his answer, and the deliberating motors sound through-out the scene.*)

ATTORNEY BRECK

Pul . . . lead . . . errrr . . . (*As if the motors are having trouble starting*) Pul . . . pul . . . lead . . . er . . . err . . . Guilty! (*Motors get it together and move in proper synchronization.*) Pul . . . Plead guilty, it's your only chance. Just plead guilty, brother. Just plead guilty. It's your only chance. Your only chance.

COURT ROYAL

Guilty? Of what? What are you talking about? What kind of defense atty are you? I don't even know what I'm being charged with, and you say plead guilty. What's happening here? (*At* VOICE) Can't I even know the charge?

>VOICE
>We told you the charge.
>Harboring a murderer.

COURT ROYAL

But that's an obvious mistake.

ATTORNEY BRECK

There's no mistake. Plead guilty. Get off easy. Otherwise *thrrrrit.* (*Makes throat-cutting gesture, then chuck-les*) Plead guilty, brother, it's your only chance. (*Laughs*)

>VOICE
>Plea changed to
>guilty?

COURT ROYAL

What? No. I'm not pleading guilty. And I want my lawyer.

> VOICE
> You have yr law-
> yer

COURT ROYAL
No, my lawyer is John Breck.

ATTORNEY BRECK
Mr. Royal, look at me. (*Grabs him by the shoulders*) I am
John Breck. (*Laughs*) Your attorney and friend. And
I say plead guilty.

COURT ROYAL
John Bre . . . what? (*He looks at* ATTORNEY *closely.*)
Breck. Great God, what's happened to you? Why do
you look like this?

ATTORNEY BRECK
Why? Haha, I've always looked like this, Mr. Royal.
Always. (*Now another voice, strong, young, begins to
shout in the darkness at* COURT.)

YOUNG VICTIM
Now will you believe me stupid fool? Will you believe what
I tell you or your eyes? Even your eyes. You're here
with me, with us, all of us, and you can't understand.
Plead guilty you are guilty stupid nigger. You'll die
they'll kill you and you don't know why now will you
believe me? Believe me, half-white coward. Will you believe reality?

> VOICE
> Get that criminal out
> of here. Beat him. Shut him
> up. Get him.

(*Now sounds of scuffling come out of darkness. Screams.
Of a group of men subduing another man.*)

YOUNG VICTIM
You bastard. And you Court Royal you let them take me.

You liar. You weakling, You woman in the face of degenerates. You let me be taken. How can you walk the earttttttt ... (*He is apparently taken away.*)

COURT ROYAL

Who's that? (*Peers into darkness*) Who's that talking to me?

VOICE
Shutup, Royal.
Fix your plea. Let's
get on with it.

COURT ROYAL

That voice sounded very familiar. (*Caught in thought momentarily*) I almost thought it was ...

VOICE
Since you keep
your plea of not
guilty you won't need a
lawyer. We can proceed without
your services, counselor.

ATTORNEY BRECK

As you wish, your honor. Goodbye, Mr. Royal. (*He begins to crawl off.*) Goodbye, dead sucker! Hahahaha. (*Waving hands as he crawls off and laughing*) Hahahaha, ain't I a bitch ... I mean ain't I? (*Exits*)

COURT ROYAL

John, John. You're my attorney, you can't leave me here like this. (*Starts after him, shouts*) JOHN! *A siren begins to scream, like in jailbreak pictures . . . "Arrrrrrrerrrrr." The lights beat off, on, in time with the metallic siren shriek.* COURT *is stopped in his tracks, bent in anticipation; the siren continues. Machine guns begin to bang bang as if very close to him, cell doors slamming, whistles, yells: "Break . . . Break!" The machine guns chatter,* COURT *stands frozen, half-bent arms held away from his body, balancing him in his terror. As the noise, din, continues, his eyes grow until he is almost going to faint.)*

Ahhhhhhgggg. Please . . . Please . . . don't kill me. Don't shoot me, I didn't do anything. I'm not trying to escape. Please . . . Please PLEEEEEAS . . .

(The VOICE *begins to shriek almost as loud with laughter as all the other sounds and jumping lights stop as* VOICE *starts to laugh. The* VOICE *just laughs and laughs, laughs until you think it will explode or spit up blood; it laughs long and eerily out of the darkness.*

(Still dazed and staggered, he looks around quickly, trying to get himself together. He speaks now very quietly, and shaken.) Please. Please. *(The other* VOICE *begins to subside, the laughs coming in sharp cut-off bursts of hysteria.)*

> VOICE
>
> You donkey. *(Laughs)*
> You piece of wood. You
> shiny shuffling piece
> of black vomit.

(The laughter quits like the tide rolling softly back to silence. Now there is no sound, except for COURT ROYAL's *breathing, and shivering clothes. He whispers . . .)*

COURT ROYAL

Please? *(He is completely shaken and defeated, frightened like a small animal, eyes barely rolling.)* Please. I won't escape. *(His words sound corny tinny stupid dropped in such silence.)* Please I won't try again. Just tell me where I am. *(The silence again. For a while no movement.* COURT *is frozen, stiff, with only eyes sneaking; now they stop, he's frozen, cannot move staring off into the cold darkness.*

(*A chain, slightly, more, now heavier, dragged bent, wiggled slowly, light now heavily in the darkness, from another direction. Chains. They're dragged, like things are pulling them across the earth. The chains. And now low chanting voices, moaning, with incredible pain and despair, the voices press just softly behind the chains, for a few seconds, so very very briefly then gone. And silence.*

(court *does not move. His eyes roll a little back and around. He bends his knees, dipping his head, bending. He moans.*)

COURT ROYAL
Just tell me where I am.

VOICE
HEAVEN.

(*The* voice *is cool and businesslike.* court's *eyes and head raise an imperceptible trifle. He begins to pull his arms slowly to his sides, and claps them together. The lights dim, and only* court *is seen in dimmer illumination. The* voice *again . . .*)

VOICE
HEAVEN.
(*Pause*)
WELCOME.

COURT ROYAL
(*Mumbling*) I never understood . . . these things are so confusing. (*His head jerks like he's suddenly heard Albert Ayler. It raises, his whole body jerks around like suddenly animate ragdoll. He does a weird dance like a marionette jiggling and waggling.*) You'll wonder what the devil-meant. A jiggedy bobbidy fool. You'll wonder what the devil-sent. Diggedy dobbidy cool. Ah man. (*Singing*) Ah man, you'll wonder who the devil-sent.

And what was heaven heaven heaven. (*This is like a funny joke-dance, with sudden funniness from* COURT; *then suddenly as before he stops frozen again, eyes rolling, no other sound heard.* . . .

Now a scream, and white hooded men push a greasy-head nigger lady across in front of COURT. *They are pulling her hair, and feeling her ass. One whispers from time to time in her ear. She screams and bites occasionally, occasionally kicking.*)

HOOD 1
(*To the* VOICE) She's drunk. (*Now to* COURT) You want to smell her breath?

COURT ROYAL
(*Frightened, also sickened at the sight, embarrassed*) N-no. I don't want to. I smell it from here. She drinks and stinks and brings our whole race down.

HOOD 2
Ain't it the truth!

VOICE
Grind her into
poison jelly.
Smear it on her
daughter's head.

HOOD 1
Right, yr honor. You got a break, sister. (*They go off.*) Hey, uncle, you sure you don't want to smell her breath?

COURT ROYAL
(*Shivers*) No.

VOICE
Royal, you have
concealed a murderer,

> and we have your punish-
> ment ready for you. Are you
> ready?

COURT ROYAL

What? No. I want a trial. Please a trial. I deserve that.
I'm a good man.

> VOICE
> Royal, you're not a
> man!

COURT ROYAL

Please . . . (*Voice breaking*) your honor, a trial. A simple
one, very quick, nothing fancy . . . I'm very conservative
. . . no frills or loud colors, a simple concrete black toilet
paper trial.

> VOICE
> And funeral.

(*Now two men in hoods, white work gloves, business suits,
very sporty, come in with a stretcher. A black man is
dead on it. There is long very piped applause. "Yea.
Yea."*)

HOOD 1

It's the Prince, yr honor. We banged him down.

> VOICE
> He's dead?

HOOD 2

Yes. A nigger did it for us.

> VOICE
> Conceal the body
> in a stone. And sink the stone
> deep under the ocean. Call the
> newspapers and give the official history.
> Make sure his voice is in that stone too, or . . .
> (*Heavy nervous pause*) Just go ahead.

HOOD 1
Of course, your honor. (*Looks to* COURT, *almost as an afterthought*) You want to smell his breath? (*They go out.*)

COURT ROYAL
(*Mumbling, still very frightened*) No ... no ... I have nothing to do with any of this. I'm a good man. I have a car. A home. (*Running down*) A club. (*Looks up, pleading*) Please there's some mistake. Isn't there? I've done nothing wrong. I have a family. I work in the Post Office, I'm a supervisor. I've worked for thirty-five years. I've done nothing wrong.

VOICE
Shutup, whimpering pig. Shutup and get ready for sentencing. It'll be hard on you, you can bet that.

COURT ROYAL
(*A little life; he sees he's faced with danger.*) But tell me what I've done. I can remember no criminal, no murderer I've housed. I work eight hours, then home, and television, dinner, then bowling. I've harbored no murderers. I don't know any. I'm a good man.

VOICE
Shutup, liar. Do you know this man?

(*An image is flashed on the screen behind him. It is a rapidly shifting series of faces. Malcolm. Patrice. Rev. King. Garvey. Dead nigger kids killed by the police. Medgar Evers*)

COURT ROYAL
What?

                              VOICE
                     I asked you do you know
                     this man? I'm asking again,
                     for the last time. There's no
                     need to lie.

COURT ROYAL
But this is many men, many faces. They shift so fast I
cannot tell who they are . . . or what is meant. It's so
confusing.

                              VOICE
                     Don't lie, Royal. We know
                     all about you. You are guilty.
                     Look at that face. You know this man.

COURT ROYAL
I do? (*In rising terror*) No. No. I don't I never saw that
man, it's so many faces, I've never seen those faces . . .
never . . .

                              VOICE
                     Look closer, Royal. You cannot
                     get away with what you've done. Look
                     more closely. You recognize
                     that face . . . don't you? The face
                     of the murderer you've sheltered all
                     these years. Look, you liar, look at
                     that face.

COURT ROYAL
No, no, no . . . I don't know them. I can't be forced into
admitting something I never did. Uhhh . . . I have
worked. My God, I've worked. I've meant to do the
right thing. I've tried to be a . . .

(*The faces shift, a long slow wail, like moan, like secret
screaming, has underscored the flashing faces. Now it
rises sharply to screaming point thrusts.* COURT *wheels*

*around to face the image on the screen, directly. He
begins shouting loud as the voices.*)

No, I've tried . . . please I never wanted anything but
peace . . . please, I tried to be a man. I did. I lost my . . .
heart . . . please it was so deep, I wanted to do the right
thing, just to do the right thing. I wanted . . . everything
to be . . . all right. Oh, please . . . please.

> VOICE
> Now tell me, whether you
> know that murderer's face or not.
> Tell me before you die!

COURT ROYAL
No, no. I don't know him. I don't. I want to do the right
thing. I don't know them. (*Raises his hands in his
agony*) Oh, son . . . son . . . dear God, my flesh, forgive
me . . . (*Begins to weep and shake*) My sons. (*He
clutches his body, shaken throughout by his ugly sobs.*)

Dear god . . .

> VOICE
> Just as we thought. You are
> the one. And you must be sentenced.

COURT ROYAL
I must be sentenced. I am the one. (*Almost trance-like*) I
must be sentenced. With the murderer. I am the one.

> VOICE
> The murderer is dead. You
> must be sentenced alone.

COURT ROYAL
(*As first realization*) The murderer . . . is . . . dead?

> VOICE
> And you must be sentenced.
> Now. Alone.

COURT ROYAL
(*Voice rising, in panic, but catching it up short*) The
murderer ... is dead.

VOICE
Yes. And your sentence is ...

COURT ROYAL
I must be sentenced ... alone. Where is the murderer?
Where is his corpse?

VOICE
You will see it presently.

COURT ROYAL
(*Head bowed*) God. And I am now to die like the murderer died?

VOICE
No. (*Long pause*) We have
decided to spare you. We admire
your spirit. It is a compliment to
know you can see the clearness of your
fate, and the rightness of it. That you
love the beauty of the way of life you've
chosen here in the anonymous world. No one
beautiful is guilty. So how can you be? All the
guilty have been punished. Or are being punished. You
are absolved of your crime, at this moment, because
of your infinite understanding of the compassionate
God Of The Cross. Whose head was cut off for you, to
absolve you of your weakness. The murderer is dead.
The murderer is dead.

(*Applause from the darkness*)

COURT ROYAL
And I am not guilty now?

VOICE
No you are free. Forever.
It is asked only that you give the final
instruction.

COURT ROYAL
Final instruction . . . I don't understand . . .

VOICE
Heroes! bring the last issue in.

(*The last two hooded men,* HOODS 3 *and* 4, *return with a young black man of about twenty. The boy does not look up. He walks stiff-legged to the center in front of* COURT. *He wears a large ankh around his neck. His head comes up slowly. He looks into* COURT'S *face.*)

YOUNG VICTIM
Peace.

COURT ROYAL
(*Looks at his face, begins to draw back. The hooded man comes and places his arms around* COURT'S *shoulders.*)

VOICE
Give him the instruction instrument.

(*Hooded man takes a pistol out of his pocket and gives it with great show to* COURT.)

HOOD 3
The silver bullet is in the chamber. The gun is made of diamonds and gold.

HOOD 4
You get to keep it after the ceremony.

VOICE
And now, with the rite of instruction, the last bit of guilt falls from you as if it was never there, Court Royal. Now, at last, you can go free.
Perform the rite, Court Royal, the final instruction.

COURT ROYAL
What? No. I don't understand.

> VOICE
The final instruction is the death of
the murderer. The murderer is dead and must
die, with each gift of our God. This gift is the
cleansing of guilt, and the bestowal of freedom.

COURT ROYAL
But you told me the murderer was dead, already.

> VOICE
It *is* already. The
murderer has been sentenced. You have
only to carry out the rite.

COURT ROYAL
But you told me the murderer was dead. (*Starts to back
away*) You told me . . . you said I would be sentenced
alone.

> VOICE
The murderer *is dead*. This
is his shadow. This one is not real.
This is the myth of the murderer. His last
fleeting astral projection. It is the murderer's
myth that we ask you to instruct. To bind it forever
. . . with death.

COURT ROYAL
I don't . . . Why do . . . you said I was not guilty. That
my guilt had fallen away.

> VOICE
The rite must be finished. This
ghost must be lost in cold space.
Court Royal, this is your destiny.
This act was done by you a million
years ago. This is only the memory of it.
This is only a rite. You cannot kill a shadow,
a fleeting bit of light and memory. This is only

a rite, to show that you would be guilty but for the cleansing rite. The shadow is killed in place of the killer. The shadow for reality. So reality can exist beautiful like it is. This is your destiny, and your already lived-out life. Instruct, Court Royal, as the centuries pass, and bring you back to your natural reality. Without guilt. Without shame. Pure and blameless, your soul washed (*Pause*) white as snow.

COURT ROYAL
(*Falling to his knees, arms extended as in loving prayer, to a bright light falling on him, racing around the space*) Oh, yes . . . I hear you. And I have waited, for this promise to be fulfilled.

VOICE
This is the fulfillment.
You must, at this moment, enter into the covenant of guiltless silence. Perform the rite, Court Royal.

COURT ROYAL
Oh, yes, yes . . . I want so much to be happy . . . and relaxed.

VOICE
Then carry out your destiny . . .

COURT ROYAL
Yes, yes . . . I will . . . I will be happy . . . (*He rises, pointing the gun straight up at the young man's face.*) I must be . . . fulfilled . . . I will. (*He fires the weapon into the boy's face. One short sound comes from the boy's mouth.*)

YOUNG VICTIM
Papa. (*He falls.*)

COURT ROYAL
(*Stands looking at the dead boy with the gun still up. He is motionless.*)

VOICE
Case dismissed, Court Royal . . . you are free.

COURT ROYAL
(*Now suddenly to life, the lights go up full, he has the gun in his hand. He drops, flings it away from him.*) My soul is as white as snow. (*He wanders up to the body.*) My soul is as white as snow. (*He starts to wander off the stage.*) White as snow. I'm free. I'm free. My life is a beautiful thing.

(*He mopes slowly toward the edge of the stage, then suddenly a brighter mood strikes him. Raising his hand as if calling someone*) Hey, Louise, have you seen my bowling bag? I'm going down to the alley for a minute. (*He is frozen, the lights dim to BLACK.*)

Madheart

(A Morality Play)

1966

For the brothers and sisters of
the Black Arts Alliance, San Francisco

Madheart was first performed at San Francisco State College in May 1967, with the following cast from the Black Arts Alliance:

Black Man, late twenties, early thirties　　Jimmy Garrett

Black Woman, twenties, with soft natural hair
caught up in gele　　　　　　　　　Velma Mitchell

Mother, black woman, in her fifties,
business suit, red wig, tipsy　　　　Yolande Redfurd

Sister, black woman, in her twenties,
mod style clothes, blond wig

Devil Lady, female with an elaborately carved
white devil mask　　　　　　　　　Elendar Barnes

The production was directed by LeRoi Jones.

Madheart was first published by William Morrow & Co., Inc. in BLACK FIRE, an Anthology of Afro-American writing, copyright © 1968 by LeRoi Jones and Larry Neal.

DEVIL LADY
You need pain. (*Coming out of shadows with neon torch, honky-tonk calliope music*) You need pain, ol' nigger devil, pure pain, to clarify your desire.

BLACK MAN
(*Turns slowly to look at her, raises his arms, straight out, parallel to the floor, then swiftly above his head, then wide open in the traditional gesture of peace*) God is not the devil. Rain is not fire nor snow, nor old women dying in hallways.

DEVIL LADY
There is peace.

BLACK MAN
There is no peace.

DEVIL LADY
There is beauty.

BLACK MAN
None that you would know about.

DEVIL LADY
There is horror.

BLACK MAN
There is horror. There is (*Pause, as if to cry or precipitate a rush of words which do not come*) . . . only horror. Only stupidity. (*Raising to point at her*) Your stale pussy weeps paper roses.

DEVIL LADY
And horror.

BLACK MAN
Why aren't you dead? Why aren't you a deader thing than nothing is?

DEVIL LADY
I am dead and can never die.

BLACK MAN
You will die only when I kill you. I raise my hand to
strike. (*Pulling out sword*) I raise my hand to strike.
Strike. Strike. (*Waving the sword, and leaping great leap*)
Bitch devil in the whistling bowels of the wind. Blind
snow creature. (*A fanfare of drums. Loud dissonant
horns. The action freezes. The lights dim slowly, on the
frozen scene. The actors fixed. The music rises. Lights
completely off. Then flash. On. On. Off. Off. As if it was
an SOS signal. Then the music changes, to a slow, insinuating, nasty blues. Rock. Rock. Voices offstage begin to
pick up the beat, and raise it to falsetto howl. Scream, in
the sensual moan*)

VOICES
Rock. Rock. Love. Me. Love. Me. Rock. Heaven. Heaven.
Ecstasy. Ecstasy. Ooooahhhhummmmah-ah-ahoooooh.
Let love. Let rock. Let Heaven. All love. All love, like
rock . . . (*Lights go full up. Silence. The action continues.
The actors from the freeze go to life, but never complete
the initial action. As if in slow motion*)

BLACK MAN
Hear that? Hear those wild cries? Souls on fire. Fire.
Floods of flame. Hear that. Ol' humanless bitch. Dead
judge.

DEVIL LADY
I am the judge. I am the judge. (*She squats like old
Chinese.*) The judge. (*Rolls on her back, with skirt
raised, to show a cardboard image of Christ pasted over
her pussy space. A cross in the background*) My pussy
rules the world through newspapers. My pussy radiates
the great heat. (*She rolls back and forth on the floor,
panting.*)

BLACK MAN
The great silence. Serenades of brutal snow. You got a cave, lady?

VOICES
Blood. Snow. Dark cold cave. Illusion. Promises. Hatred and Death. Snow. Death. Cold. Waves. Night. Dead white. Sunless. Moonless. Forever. Always. Iceberg Christians, pee in the ocean. Help us. We move. (*Music again, over all, the high beautiful falsetto of a fag. The traditional love song completely taking over. BLACKOUT.*

Lights up, the DEVIL LADY *lies in the middle of the stage with a spear, or many arrows, stuck in her stomach and hole. As the lights come up, the singing subsides to low hum. Three black women enter slowly (* MOTHER, SISTER, WOMAN), *humming now softly. The* BLACK MAN *is standing just a few feet away from the skewered* DEVIL LADY. *He is gesturing with his hands, at the prone figure, with his hands like he is conjuring or hypnotizing.*)

BLACK MAN
You will always and forever be dead, and be dead, and always you will be the spirit of deadness, or the cold stones of its promise. (*He takes up a huge wooden stake and drives it suddenly into her heart, with a loud thud as it penetrates the body, and crashes deep in the floor.*) Beautiful. (*Preoccupied, and still unaware of the black women*) Beautiful. (*He makes as if to repeat his act, and one of the women speaks.*)

MOTHER
No. Madman. Stop!

SISTER
She is old and knows. Her wisdom inherits the earth. (*Stepping forward suddenly at* DEVIL LADY) I love you. I love the woman in my sleep. I cannot love death.

BLACK WOMAN
Perhaps we are intruding. (*The two other women turn and stare at her, and form a quick back-off circle to point at her casually and turn their heads. The* BLACK WOMAN'S *head is wrapped in a modest gele, and her natural hair cushions her face in a soft remark.*) You want the whole thing.

MOTHER
You want the whole thing, baby. (*Advancing*) The earth, the sky.

SISTER
You must leave what the womb leaves. The possibility of all creation.

BLACK MAN
The dead do not sing. Except through the sawdust lips of science-fiction jigaboos, who were born, and disappeared, in a puff of silence at the foot of the Woolworth heir's cement condom.

DEVIL LADY
(*From the floor, moaning through her teeth, from beyond the grave. Let there be music, and setting, to indicate that these words come from behind the veil.*) OOOOOOOO-AHHHHHHHH . . . My pussy throbs above the oceans, forcing weather into the world.

BLACK MAN
The cold.

MOTHER
The light and promise. (*From an ecstatic pose, suddenly turns into a barker, selling young black ass*) Uhyehhh. Eh? Step right up. Get your free ass. (*Starts moving wiggle—suggestively*) Come on, fellahs . . .

SISTER
And free enterprise.

DEVIL LADY
Enter the prize. And I am the prize. And I am dead. And
all my life is me. Flowing from my vast whole, entire
civilizations.

BLACK WOMAN
(*Almost inadvertently*) That smell. I knew I'd caught
it before.

BLACK MAN
Broomsticks thrust up there return embossed with zom-
bie gold.

MOTHER
Out of the bowels of the sun. I slap around drunk up
Lenox. Stumble down 125th into the poet who frowns at
me, lost in my ways. You'd think that ol' nigger was
worth something.

SISTER
(*Dazed*) It's just . . . just . . . (*Staggers toward the dead
woman*) . . . that I wanted to be something like her, that's
all. (*Weeps but tries to hold it*)

BLACK WOMAN
Yet she be a stone beast, ladies! A stone ugly pagan.
Israelites measure your beauty by what the filthy bitch
looks like lying around like an old sore.

BLACK MAN
An old punctured sore with the pus rolled out.

SISTER
(*Falling to her knees. Screams*) Aiiiieeeee . . . it could be
me, that figure on the floor. It could be me, and backward
out of the newspaper dreams of my American life. Out of
the television enemas poured through my eyes out my
mouth onto the floor of everybody's life. I hate so. I am in
love with my hatred. Yet I worship this beast on the floor,
because . . .

BLACK WOMAN
Because you have been taught to love her by background
music of sentimental movies. A woman's mind must be
stronger than that.

BLACK MAN
A black woman. (*Throws his hands above his head*) A
black woman! Wouldn't that be something? (*The dead
white woman's body wiggles in a shudder and releases,
dead.*)

BLACK WOMAN
(*Her voice goes up to high long sustained note.*) I am
black black and am the most beautiful thing on the planet.
Touch me if you dare. I am your soul.

MOTHER
What is wrong with the niggers, this time? I'm old and I
hump along under my wig. I'm dying of oldness. I'm dying
of the weight. The air is so heavy. (*Taken by more som-
ber mood*) And dying all the time. Diseased. Broken.
Sucking air from dirty places. Your mother. Shit filthi-
ness. In a cheap mink. In a frozen roach funeral.

SISTER
Brazen bitch. You trying to steal my shit?

MOTHER
Make for the exit, child, before you bleed on somebody.
(*They begin to have at each other. Breathing hard and
cursing. The* BLACK WOMAN *backs away, hands at her
mouth, terrified.*)

BLACK WOMAN
(*Coming close to the* BLACK MAN, *as the two women begin to fight in aggravated pantomimed silence. Clock
gongs away, maybe fifty times. Slow sudden insinuating
drums, and brushes. The two women fighting clutch each
other and fight more stiffly, finally subsiding into a frozen*

posture.) What do you want, black man? What can I give you? (*In a calm loving voice*) Is there a heart bigger than mine? Is there any flesh sweeter, any lips fatter and redder, any thighs more full of orgasms?

BLACK MAN
(*Leaning toward her*) Sweet pleasure. (*He touches her arm*.)

DEVIL LADY
(*Beginning to moan on the floor*) Oooooooooooooooooo-aaaaaaaaaa. My white pussy is beating, the air. My navel is raw and ready to be attached. I come back from the dead 'cause I wanna.

BLACK MAN
Oh, bullshit. Go back, for chrissakes.

BLACK WOMAN
Christ was a pagan. A stumblebum in the Swedish baths of philosophy. (*The two women struggle suddenly on the floor. With violence and slobbering*)

TWO WOMEN
Fuckingbitch Fuckingbitch Fuckingbitch Fuckingbitch
Fuckingbitch Fuckingbitch Fuckingbitch Fuckingbitch
Fuckingbitch Fuckingbitch Fuckingbitch . . .

BLACK WOMAN
Thing on the floor, be still. I'm tired of your ignorant shamble. Let me be alone in the world with women and men, and your kind be still in the grave where you have fun. (DEVIL LADY *screams with throbbing thighs*. MOTHER *and* SISTER *begin crawling across the floor to the* DEVIL LADY. *She writhes and stiffens in death. The* MOTHER *whimpers, the* SISTER *gags and weeps and whines*.)

SISTER
My dead sister reflection. Television music. Soft lights and soft living among the buildings.

BLACK WOMAN
She went for luxury.

BLACK MAN
I used to see her in white discothèque boots and sailor pants. (*Pointing to the crawling women*) This is the nightmare in all of our hearts. Our mothers and sisters groveling to white women, wanting to be white women, dead and hardly breathing on the floor. Look at our women dirtying themselves. (*Runs and grabs wig off* SISTER's *head*) Take off filth. (*He throws it onto the dead woman's body.*) Take your animal fur, heathen. (*Laughs*) Heathen. Heathen. I've made a new meaning. Let the audience think about themselves, and about their lives when they leave this happening. This black world of purest possibility. (*Laughs*) All our lives we want to be alive. We scream for life.

BLACK WOMAN
Be alive, black man. Be alive, for me. For me, black man. (*Kisses him*) And love me. Love, Me.

BLACK MAN
Women, assemble around me. I'm gonna sing for you now, in my cool inimitable style. About my life. About my road, and where it's taking me now. Assemble, sweet black ladies, ignorant or true, and let me run down the game of life.

BLACK WOMAN
Get up, you other women, and listen to your man. This is no fattening insurance nigger graying around the temples. This is the soulforce of our day-to-day happening universe. A man.

SISTER
A man. Dammit. Dance. (*Change*) Men. What do they do? Hang out. Niggermen. If I have to have a niggerman, give me a faggot anyday.

MOTHER
(*Laughing high voice and sweeping her hand*) Oh, chil',
I know the kind you mean. Uhh, so sweet. I tell you. But
. . . a white boy's better, daughter. Don't you forget it.
Just as sof' and sweet as a pimple. (*Spies* BLACK WOMAN
*still standing separate and looking confused, hands cover-
ing her ears*) Haha . . . (*Hunching or trying to hunch*
SISTER) Haaha, will you look at that simple bitch. My
lan', chil', why don't you straighten up and get in the
world?

SISTER
Yeh, Desideria, why don't you make up your mind?

BLACK MAN
What is this? (*To* BLACK WOMAN) What's all this mouth
mouth action? Why don't these women act like women
should? Why don't they act like Black Women? All this
silly rapping and screaming on the floor. I should turn
them over to the Black Arts and get their heads relined.

BLACK WOMAN
They've been tricked and gestured over. They hypnotized,
that's all. White Magic.

BLACK MAN
White Magic. Yes. (*Raising his stake, suddenly*) Maybe
this dead thing's fumes are sickening the air. I'll make
sure it's dead. (*He strikes.*)

SISTER
(*Screams as* BLACK MAN *stabs the* DEVIL LADY. *Grabs her
heart as if the man had struck her*) Oh God, you've killed
me, nigger.

BLACK MAN
What? (*Wheels to look at her*)

BLACK WOMAN
You're killed if you are made in the dead thing's image,

if the dead thing on the floor has your flesh, and your soul.
If you are a cancerous growth. Sad thing.

SISTER

I'm killed and in horrible agony, and my own brother did
it. (*Staggering around stage. Finally falls in great over-
dramatic climax*) My own bro . . . ther. (*Falls*)

BLACK MAN

Oh, God! (*Rushes over to her*) Is this child my sister?

BLACK WOMAN

No, get away from her. She is befouled.

BLACK MAN

But my own sister . . . I've killed her.

BLACK WOMAN

She's not even dead. She just thinks she has to die because that white woman died. She's sick.

BLACK MAN

(*Stands over* SISTER, *pondering what the* BLACK WOMAN
has said) Hmmmmmm.

MOTHER

You've killed her. You've killed my baby. (*Rushes over to*
BLACK MAN *and starts beating him in the chest. She's
weeping loud and disconsolately.*) You've killed my own
sweet innocent girl. My own sweet innocent girl . . . she
never had a chance. She coulda been somebody.

BLACK WOMAN

Woman, you're crazy.

BLACK MAN

I killed my sister. (*Mumbling*)

MOTHER

No, I'm not the crazy one. You all are crazy. Stuntin' like
this. All that make-believe. And you killed your own flesh.

And this ol' nappy-head bitch agitated the whole shit.
(*Weeps*) My baby, she never had a chance. She never
even got a chance to be nobody. Oh, God, why's my life
so fucked up? And you, man, you killed your own sister.
I hope that shit you talk's enough to satisfy you. Or that
nappy-head bitch.

BLACK WOMAN
Why don't you find out something before you show how
long ignorance can claim a body? An old woman like you
should be wise . . . but you not wise worth a mustard
seed.

MOTHER
You talk to me with respect, whore . . . or I'll . . . (*Threatening gesture*)

BLACK WOMAN
What? Or you'll beat me with your wig? You're streaked
like the devil. And that pitiful daughter of yours is not
even dead. But she'll act dead as long as she licks on that
devil woman.

BLACK MAN
My mother, my sister, both . . . like television dollbabies,
doing they ugly thing. To mean then, me, and what they
have for me, what I be then, in spite my singing, and
song, to stand there, or lay there, like they be, with the
horizon blowing both ways, to change, God damn . . . and
be a weight around my neck . . . a weight . . .

MOTHER
Well, leave us alone, murderer . . . punk ass murderer.
Gimme a drink an' shut up. And drag that whore's mouth
shut too.

BLACK WOMAN
You shut up. And get back in your dead corner with the
other rotting meat.

BLACK MAN
I've killed my sister. And now watch my mother defiled, thrown in a corner.

BLACK WOMAN
If she was your mother, she'd be black like you. She'd come at you to talk to you, about old south, and ladies under trees, and the soft wet kiss of her own love, how it made you fight through sperm to arrive on this planet whole . . . (*Soft laugh*) . . . and beautiful.

BLACK MAN
Who're you . . . to talk so much . . . and to stand apart from this other jive? The lousy score's two to one, diddy-bops! (MOTHER *starts singing a sad dirge for the daughter, trailing around the body, throwing kisses at the still figures.*)

MOTHER
Yohoooooo yohoooooo, daw daw daw daw daw daw daw yodaw hoooodaw deee. All the beauty we missed. All the cool shit. All the sad drinking in crummy bars we missed. All the crossmating and crossbreeding and holy jive in the cellars and closets. The cool flirts in the ladies' meeting. The meeting of the ex-wives. All the Belafontes and Poitiers and hid unfamous nigger formers, hip still on their lawns, and corn and wine, and tippy drinks with green stuff with cherries and white cats with titles, all the television stuff, and tapdances, and the soft music, and stuff. All of it gone. Dead child, save me, or take me . . . (*She bows, kisses the two bodies.*) Or save me, take me with you . . . Daw daw dooooodaw daw ding ding daw do do dooon . . . (*She trails sadly around the bodies.*)

BLACK MAN
This is horrible. Look at this.

BLACK WOMAN
It's what the devil's made. You know that. Why don't you

stop pretending the world's a dream or puzzle? I'm real and whole . . . (*Holds out her arms*) And yours, only, yours, but only as a man will you know that.

BLACK MAN
You are . . .

BLACK WOMAN
I'm the black woman. The one who disappeared. The sleepwalker. The one who runs through your dreams with your life and your seed. I am the black woman. The one you need. You know this. Now you must discover a way to get me back, Black Man. You and you alone, must get me. Or you'll never . . . lord . . . be a man. My man. Never know your own life needs. You'll walk around white ladies breathing their stink, and lose your seed, your future to them.

BLACK MAN
I'll get you back. If I need to.

BLACK WOMAN
(*Laughs*) You need to, baby . . . just look around you. You better get me back, if you know what's good for you . . . you better.

BLACK MAN
(*Looking around at her squarely, he advances.*) I better? . . . (*A soft laugh*) Yes. Now is where we always are . . . that now . . . (*He wheels and suddenly slaps her crosswise, back and forth across the face.*)

BLACK WOMAN
Wha . . . What . . . oh love . . . please . . . don't hit me. (*He hits her, slaps her again.*)

BLACK MAN
I want you, woman, as a woman. Go down. (*He slaps again.*) Go down, submit, submit . . . to love . . . and to man, now, forever.

BLACK WOMAN
(*Weeping, turning her head from side to side*) Please don't hit me . . . please . . . (*She bends.*) The years are so long, without you, man, I've waited . . . waited for you . . .

BLACK MAN
And I've waited.

BLACK WOMAN
I've seen you humbled, black man, seen you crawl for dogs and devils.

BLACK MAN
And I've seen you raped by savages and beasts, and bear bleach shit children of apes.

BLACK WOMAN
You permitted it . . . you could . . . do nothing.

BLACK MAN
But now I can. (*He slaps her, drags her to him, kissing her deeply on the lips.*) That shit is ended, woman, you with me, and the world is mine.

BLACK WOMAN
I . . . oh love, please stay with me . . .

BLACK MAN
Submit, for love.

BLACK WOMAN
I . . . I submit. (*She goes down, weeping.*) I submit . . . for love . . . please love. (*The* MAN *sinks to his knees and embraces her, draws her with him up again. They both begin to cry and then laugh, laugh, wildly at everything and themselves.*)

BLACK MAN
You are my woman, now, forever. Black woman.

BLACK WOMAN
I am your woman, and you are the strongest of God. Fill
me with your seed. (*They embrace.* . . . MOTHER *is now
crawling around on her knees.*)

MOTHER
Tony Bennett, help us please. Beethoven, Peter Gunn . . .
deliver us in our sterling silver headdress . . . oh please
deliver us.

BLACK MAN
This is enough of this stuff. Get up, supposed-to-be
mother, and drag that supposed-to-be-sister up too. This
stuff is over and done. Get up or so help me, you die with
the dead bitch you worship.

MOTHER
What I care? Batman won't love me without my yellow-
head daughter. I'm too old for him or Robin. I can't paint
soupcans, the junk I find is just junk, my babies stick in
they eyes, I'm sick in the big world, and white shit zooms
without me. I'm a good fuck and an intelligent woman . . .
frankly . . . frankly . . . (*Laughs. Turns to look at the*
BLACK MAN) Fuck both of you stupid ass niggers . . . you'll
never get no light . . . Daughter . . . Daughter . . . put on
your wig and wake up dancing. The old Italian wants you
to marry him.

BLACK MAN
Why won't these women listen? Why do they want to die?

BLACK WOMAN
The white one's fumes strangle their senses. The thing's
not dead.

BLACK MAN
I've killed it. And death must come to the thing. I'll do it
again. (*Shouts*) Die, you bitch, and drag your mozarts
into your nasty hole. Your mozarts stravinskys stupid

white sculpture corny paintings deathfiddles, all your crawling jive, drag it in and down with you, your office-buildings blow up in your pussy, newspapers poison gases congolene brain stragglers devising ways to deal death to their people, your smiles, your logic, your brain, your intellectual death, go to a dead planet in some metal bullshit, dissolve, disappear, leave your address in the volcano, and turn into the horrible insects of a new planet . . . but leave. I am the new man of the earth, I command you . . . Command bullshit. (*He runs over and stomps the dead* DEVIL LADY *in her face.*) This kinda command. (*He drags her over to the edge of the stage, and drops her off.*) Into the pit of deadchange, slide bitch slide. (*Smoke and light shoot up where she lands.*)

BLACK WOMAN
Yes yes . . .

MOTHER
You fool. You crazy thing . . . get out of here.

BLACK WOMAN
Why don't you listen . . . or die, old hag!

BLACK MAN
(*Grabs* MOTHER *by the arm, drags her over to the edge*) Look down in there, smell those fumes. That's ashy death, bitchmother, stinking filthy death. That's what you'll be. Smell it. Look at it!

MOTHER
You fool, you mess with the gods, and shit will belt you.

BLACK WOMAN
Listen, old woman, this is a man speaking, a black man. (MAN *shakes the* MOTHER *violently.*)

BLACK MAN
Yes, you listen.

MOTHER

No, no . . . (*She pulls away, goes to* SISTER, *who's now starting to turn over, fan and shake herself.*) Get away . . . you've killed my daughter . . . you . . . what, she's still breathing?

BLACK WOMAN

I told you she was . . . "sick actress from Broome Street."

MOTHER

Oh, daughter . . . the Italian called you jest a while ago. Get up, pussycat, Mama's worried so about you. You hungry? (*She pulls out a box lunch from her brassiere.*) You must be starved.

SISTER

(*Wakes up, looks around, senses the* DEVIL LADY *is missing, dead*) Where . . . where's she . . . ooh . . . Where's my body . . . my beautiful self? Where? What'd you do, you black niggers? What'd you do to me? Where'd you hide me? Where's my body? My beautiful perfumed hole?

MOTHER

The hairy nigger killed you, daughter, dropped you in a . . . pit.

SISTER

What! OOOOOOOOOOOOO . . . (*Horrible shriek*) OOOOOOOOOO . . . here . . . ooooo . . . (*Runs toward* BLACK MAN) You beast bastard . . . OOOOOOOO . . . Where'd you stick my body . . . ? (BLACK MAN *grabs her and tosses her to the floor,* MOTHER *goes over to comfort her.*)

MOTHER

Oh, please, pussycat . . . ain't you hungry a little bit? I saved some dinner for you. Eat something, pussycat, baby, don't aggravate yourself. You'll ruin your complexion. Don't let these niggers upset you.

SISTER
Oh, God, I know . . . he's killed me. He's dropped me in
that pit. (*Weeps unconsolably*)

BLACK WOMAN
Bitchfool.

SISTER
You jealous 'cause you ain't blonde like me, nigger. You
shut up and get outta here with that nigger . . . You get
outta here . . . get outta here. So help me I'll kill you . . .
get outta here, get outta here, get outta here . . . (*Screams,
turns into mad raving creature, runs, puts wig back on
head, pulls it down over her eyes, runs around stage
screaming*, MOTHER *chasing her trying to feed her from
the box*)

MOTHER
Please . . . oh, please, baby . . . jest a little bit o' greens,
they's flavored with knuckles . . . oh, pussycat, please,
you'll be alive agin . . . that nigger can't stop you . . .
pussycat . . .

BLACK MAN
(*Stunned, staring, tears coming to his eyes. The* WOMAN
comes to comfort him.) What can I do . . . ?

BLACK WOMAN
Baby, baby . . .

BLACK MAN
My mother . . . and sister . . . crazy white things slobbering . . . God help me.

BLACK WOMAN
Oh, baby, you can't help it . . . you just can't help it. (*The
two women finally fall in the middle of the stage, holding
each other, the older woman feeding the* SISTER, *with a
spoon out of a small pot, some collard greens. The young
girl still sobs.*)

SISTER
OOOOOHhhhhhh God, God help me . . .

BLACK MAN
But this can't go, this stuff can't go. They'll die or help
us, be black or white and dead. I'll save them or kill them.
That's all. But not this shit . . . not this . . . horrible shit.
(BLACK MAN *runs over and gets firehose, brings it back
and turns it on the two women.*) Now, let's start again,
women. Let's start again. We'll see what you get . . . life
. . . or death . . . we'll see . . . (*He sprays them and they
struggle until they fall out. Then the* BLACK MAN *and*
BLACK WOMAN *stand over the two on the floor.*)

BLACK WOMAN
You think there's any chance for them? You really think
so?

BLACK MAN
They're my flesh. I'll do what I can. (*Looks at her*) We'll
both try. All of us, black people. (*Curtain*)

The End

WHY NO J-E-L-L-O ?

In an era when Lyndon Johnson is accused in a dumb joke evenings of having knocked off the first Kennedy, and Maddox is molested by Jewish liberals for having had the honesty to be the true devil that they all are, this publisher has the nerve to censor and refuse to publish the play, J-E-L-L-O, as attacking a public figure's private life.

It sound seems like something shaky in the state of white head. How this is figured we can tell right off. This play J-E-L-L-O has been censored, kept off the set for all the years since its writing (1965) except that its been seen by more Black People than most plays, aside, unfortunately, from the tv sets, because this was one of the plays we took out into the streets in harlem and in other streets across the country.

So the paradox is that 666 is keeping the truth as usual from him self, but he is the truth of this play's hypotheses so nuff sd. Except the play is about Jack Benny and Rochester, and what happens when Rochester digs hisself. Can you dig it.

But have no fear Jihad is publishing the play as a side order, and this like is no protest, but an advertisement.

Adzhu Billahi Mini Shaitani
R Rajim

Ameer Baraka